Hilarious Jokes For Funny People: Jokes & Spaghetti: 27th Joke Book:

Maverick Ashley Lenartson, Ph.D Comedy

If I was a cookie I'd be a **Whoreo** with a lot of creamy white filling to lick out

IF YOU WERE
A COOKIE,
YOU'D BE A
WHOREO

Go Nads, Go Nads, Go Nads...Go Nads, Go Nads, Go Nads...

Sunbathing your butthole is the latest wellness trend Influencers swear by: it used to be the anus bleaching but, I say butt now that has been replaced by the sunbathing.

The Thanksgiving Turkey said, "I want you to know I was watching porn so I'll be extra moist."

At a wedding reception I attended recently someone said, "All the married men stand next to the person who has made your life worth living." The bartender was nearly crushed to death!!!

What exactly are **CASUAL ENCOUNTERS OF THE ANONYMOUS KIND**: Close Encounters of The Third Kind with humans not Aliens!

Playing around with the gerbils: that's an Urban Myth: who in their right mind wood want a gerbil up their asshole: I surely woodn't

Manhunt is a bunch of Trolls trolling each other online looking for hot anonymous sex w/ each other: I think I'm going to find something better to do than cruise for sex online with fat, ugly older men.

Did you have a good time in there??? No, they're just a bunch of **Ferries** in there honey my good friend Steven said about going to a **Gay Bar**. That's how he seduces "straight" cab drivers when they take him home, if he's interested in them at all.

"Why don'tcha come up and see me some time", "Is that a rocket in your pocket or are you just happy to see me???" – **Mae West**

Donnie Frank: he had manboobs as a man when growing up!!!

Complement = Cumpliment

No Ordinary Boy...ha ha ha ha ha...well, that is true FOR ME, not anybody else: "I'm no ordinary boy..."

My friend's father, Donald Carini was having sex w/ his wife, Fay Bowker Carini and put his finger down in ass crack to check for cleanliness. There was a turd on it and he just wiped it on the white bed sheets and went back to having sex w/ his wife Fay. She was disgusted to say the least.

Dawgfriendlyguy
VERY LUCKY: I don't have to look at "Tacky Queens"...ha ha ha ha ha...
MaverickDiamond

Who wants to look at tacky Queens anyways??? I'd rather look at straight men who want their dicks sucked dry. Then right after they're done coming in my mouth or butt they leave: no relationship needed. Ahh, the Gay Life.

Excised = Sexcited

Astroglide = Assholeglide, Kuntholeglide, Moutholeglide, etc.

At least I'm not a woah!man w/ perky tits as then I might be transgendered or just a woman with flat mole hills...**HA! HA!**

Tickle Me Elmo _IS_ the doll to get somebody who **<u>HATES</u>** themselves!!! Maybe **Tickle Me Elmo** will get them out of their deep funk!!!

Circa = Circus

MaybeLookin4U

Nooooottttttt innntttteerrrreeessssstttteeeddddd. Do you understand?

Maverick Diamond

What's to **<u>UNDERSTAND</u>** HONEY???: Have a Happy **Black FRIDAY**. go love your self: I can't wait 'til you get fuct so hard that your girlfriend has to come pick you up at your latest trick's apartment...

MaybeLookin4U

Pathetic old man, go away
MaverickDiamond
I can't wait 'til you go to jail: have a lovely day!!!
MaverickDiamond
Why did God invent <u>YOU</u>: so that the world could become
a lot more <u>FABULOUS</u>. I'm done with your
sick rotten attitude: **BYE GIRL!!!**
MaybeLookin4U
Finally, NO REPLY AT ALL

SilverCream I 61
Crazy sexy!
MavereickDiamond
that's what **I LIKE**: I mean LIKE ME: ha ha ha ha ha ha ha:
the Internet has turned most people into slaves & trolls ...
MaverickDiamond
My **REAL** name is **Ben Dover**
SilverCream I 61
I'd like that! Bent Over & Lovin' It!!!

clip clip clip clip = clit clit clit clit

THE BIG HOUSE: what exactly IS the Big House: jail,
prison, your mama's house or your own home

The White House = The Black House

The Cum Club: The Cum Quats

Bubbles The Clown or **Bubbles** was Micheal Jackson's monkey: what does bubbles have to do w/ being a clown: Monkey's usually have big smiles on their faces.

Coopers Droop: A woman's saggy bottom breasts that go down to her waist from not wearing a bra!!!

Religious People: when they come to my door I ask them *IF* they want to discuss religion in the **NUDE**!!! It doesn't take long to get them to leave as I really don't want to hear about how I'm supposed to believe in God & convert to their way of life: I do believe in God but not when God is shoved down my throat.

HAR ASS MENT: what exactly **IS** that???!!! When somebody won't leave you alone there are two ways to get rid of them: **1.** Tell 'em you have a "Social Disease" **2.** Tell them you like it when they take a shit in your mouth or you want to take a dump in their mouth because it turns you on.

How To Get A Guy Interested In You When You Are Gay, Bi- or Straight Maverick Ashley Lenartson 198 Sherwood St 3 Portland ME 04103 **207-331-4207** Mail **34.60** for the complete goods: thanks so much: **Happy Holy Days 2019!!!**

Can' Say No Productions UnLtd.: learn how to say, "NO," & "Go LOVE Your Self." I know, I know the l o v e part sounds like I just said, "Go **FUCK** Your Self," but that's not my intention: it's my way of getting rid of people politely even though it doesn't seem polite. I'm trying not to start a cat fight war with whomever wants **<u>FREE</u>** Money or stuff out of me that they won't return anyways.

I'm a WALMART **SPECIAL** I want you to know…

ROUGH TRADE by Maverick Ashley Lenartson

A **craptop** is a computer that won't work correctly since the day you bought it and they'll crap out on you when you least expect it!!! **Caveat Emptor** – <u>BUYER BEWARE</u>!!!

Control – Janet Jackson: that's what my life is **ALL about**!!

"Don't hit Steven in the head ever **again** as he's a sensitive little boy," said Steven Carini's mother Fay to her abusive husband Donald

McDonald's: Slamburgers or Big Beef Injections

DRAGULA = DRACULA IN DRAG

SPECIAL FORCES: that would be me: treat me right or get the fuck out!!!

I'm All Man On The Outside, All Woah!man On The Inside or **All Woman On The Outside, All Man On The Inside**. Take your pick depending on who you are.

What does a guy say to another woman or a guy just before he cums??? How would I know, I'm not a guy, or how would I know, I'm not a gay, or how would I know, I'm not a woah!man: You know what they say, "I'm gonna cum!!!" Most men when they have somebody suck their dick like to pull out and look at themselves cum. Then there are the guys who like to not announce they are cumming and cum in the other person's mouth.

I'm trans all the way: yeah right: you don't look trans. Trans have all the right in Society these days. Forget about Gay People.

The Gutter Boys – Maverick Ashley Lenartson, Ph.D Sexology

Sweetser Group Homes hires fat people to be the Secretaries to answer the phones. At least that's what my friend Steven told me.

"He's too old to adjust to our ways" What was he doing, living @ the Sweetser Home for Runaway Boys??? Or, "The Animal Farm", a group home for boys, or jail???!!!

What do you call a group of Mexicans who are here illegally working here in America??? Migrant workers or house cleaners: Spic & Span some would say. Isn't that what they use to clean the floors???

Make fun of every Nationality, etc. jokes & spaghetti

The **house father** is the guy who is a priest or a married guy who takes care of the children: x-amount of children there…

You don't like antiseptic??? How about analseptic??? It's nice & clean…

What exactly **IS** a brain fart??? That's when you can't think straight and have talked about too many subjects or you've got Alzheimer's Disease & are going to slowly lose your mind from not taking Vitamin B Complex to help stop the progression of your rotting brain!!!

Did you know a guy is more likely to lick an asshole if he's been fucking it with his big phat giant cum filled cawk…

Don't pour gasoline on the fire…it will only make it worse: same goes for arguing with an asshole: just walk away!!!

You're a cocky son of a bitch, get away from me or **LEAVE ME ALONE!!!!!!!!!!!!!!!!!!!!!!!!!!!**

BABY STEPS (MY ADULT LIFE) – Maverick Ashley Lenartson

Old Data – Old Daddy that's past it's **PRIME!!!** What's a girl or a boy to do???!!!

What's My Name??? **Teletubby**

I used to live in the **Big House**: my parents owned a really big house when I was growing up.

Connection or **Connexion**: a multi-sexual bar somewhere in Portland, Maine or I'd call it **Sneakers** for guys into sniffing filthy or brand new sneakers!!!

Ashley Lenartson a true pig!!!

David P David Dee Ashley Lenartson hog said ain't nobody getting anything it's all mine!!!

Ashley Lenartson David P David Dee minezes is how they say it as they have problems w/ pronunciation as in ask = I axe u a question...

I gently slid her _ _ _ _ body into the wooden sailboat on top of a funeral pyre and set it on fire...then I gently sent it into the ocean and said my goodbyes.

                    ~~~TWELVE DAYS OF CHRISTMAS~~~

December 14, 1997

My dearest darling John:

     Whoever in the whole world would dream of getting a
real Partridge in a Pear Tree? How can I ever express my
pleasure? Thank you, a hundred times, for thinking of me
this way.

                              My love always,

                              Agnes

    ==
                    ~~~

December 15, 1997

Dearest John:

     Today the postman brought your very sweet gift.
Just imagine two turtle doves. I'm just delighted at
your very thoughtful gift. They are just adorable.

                         All my love,

                              Agnes

==

December 16, 1997

Dear John:

     Oh! Aren't you the extravagant one. Now I must
protest. I don't deserve such generosity, three French
hens. They are just darling but I must insist, you've
been too kind.

                         All my love,

                              Agnes

December 17, 1997

Dear John:

     Today the postman delivered four calling birds. Now
really, they are beautiful, but don't you think enough is
enough. You are being too romantic.

                              Affectionately,

                              Agnes

===

December 18, 1997

Dearest John:

     What a surprise. Today the postman delivered five
golden rings, one for every finger. You're just
impossible, but I love it. Frankly, all those birds
squawking were beginning to get on my nerves.

                         All my love,

                         Agnes

===

December 19, 1997

Dear John:

    When I opened the door today there were actually six
geese laying on my front steps. <u>So</u> you're back to the
birds again huh? These geese are huge. Where will I
ever keep them? The neighbors are complaining and I
can't sleep through the racket. Please stop.

                    Cordially,

                    Agnes

==

December 20, 1997

John:

    What's with you and those freaking birds?? Seven
swans a swimming. What kind of damn joke is this?
There's bird poop all over the house and they never stop
the racket. I can't sleep at night and I'm a nervous
wreck. It's not funny. <u>So</u> stop those freaking birds.

                    Sincerely,

                    Agnes

December 21, 1997

O.K. Buster:

    I think I prefer the birds. What the hell am I
going to do with 8 maids a milking? It's not enough with
all those birds and 8 maids a milking, but they had to
bring their damn cows. There is manure all over the lawn
and I can't move in my own house. Just lay off me,
smartass.

                              Agnes

===

December 22, 1997

Hey Shithead:

    What are you.....some kind of sadist? Now there's
nine pipers playing. And Christ do they play. They've
never stopped chasing those maids since they got here
yesterday morning. The cows are getting upset and
they're stepping all over those screeching birds. What
am I going to do? The neighbors have started a petition
to evict me.

                          You'll get yours!

                              Agnes

December 23, 1997

You rotten prick:

     Now there's ten ladies dancing. I don't know why I
call those sluts ladies. They've been balling those
pipers all night long. Now the cows can't sleep and
they've got diarrhea. My living room is a river of shit.
The Commissioner of Buildings has subpoenaed me to give
cause why the building shouldn't be condemned. I'm
calling the police on <u>you !</u>

                              Agnes

==

December 24, 1997

Listen Fuckhead:

     What's with those eleven lords a leaping on those
maid and ladies? Some of those broads will never walk
again. Those pipers ran through the maids and have been
committing sodomy with the cows. All twenty-three of the
birds <u>aredead</u>. They've been trampled to death in the
orgy. I hope you're satisfied, you rotten vicious swine.

                         You're sworn enemy,

                              Agnes

December 25, 1997

Dear Sir:

This is to acknowledge your latest gift of twelve
fiddlers fiddling which you have seen fit to inflict on
our client, Miss Agnes McHolstein. The destruction, of
course, was total. All correspondence should come to our
attention. If you should attempt to reach Miss
McHolstein at Happy DaleSanitarium, the attendants have
been instructed to shoot you on sight.

With this letter please find attached a warrant for your
arrest.

                    Cordially,

                    Law Offices

                        of

                    Badger, Bender and Chole

December 25, 1997

Dear Sir:

 This is to acknowledge your latest gift of twelve
fiddlers fiddling which you have seen fit to inflict on
our client, Miss Agnes McHolstein. The destruction, of
course, was total. All correspondence should come to our
attention. If you should attempt to reach Miss
McHolstein at Happy DaleSanitarium, the attendants have
been instructed to shoot you on sight.

 With this letter please find attached a warrant for your
arrest.

                    Cordially,

                    Law Offices

                       of

                    Badger, Bender and Chole

BEST thing I've seen all day longer: just what am I gunna
do w/ those darn **BIRDS OF A FEATHER**???!!! Honey,
you're welcome to come over for a feast like you won't
believe on Christmas Eve, X-Mas & more...Ta! Da! Just
HAD to copy & paste this into my next joke book I'm

finishing up before Christmas & a pix of a Christmas Wreath on a shirt...that's the **BEST!!!** I could do...Just had to copy & paste all the 12 Days of Christmas for my next joke book: I suppose I'll have to paste & copy a copy of a Christmas Tree next. Stay tuned:

X-MAS HAS BEEN CANCELLED

Ashley Lenartson I'm all about **Peace**, Prosperity **Happeniss AND** **Networking**

WITH ALL THIS SPENDING ON BLACK FRIDAY...

BETTER PAY YOUR ELECTRIC BILL OR NEXT FRIDAY WILL BE BLACK TOO!

People have to
pretend you're a
bad person so they
don't feel guilty
about the things
they did to you.

**Grammar doesn't define your intelligence.
Grades don't define your knowledge.
Your attitude defines who you are.**

The budget explained in simple English.

I love it when complex things are simplified so that we can all understand.

- United States Tax revenue: $2,170,000,000,000
- Fed budget: $3,820,000,000,000
- New debt: $1,650,000,000,000
- National debt: $14,271,000,000,000
- Recent budget cut: $38,500,000,000

Now, remove 8 zeros and pretend it's a household budget.

- Annual family income: $21,700
- Money the family spent: $38,200
- New debt on the credit card: $16,500
- Outstanding balance on credit card: $142,710
- Total budget cuts which some politicians are proud about: $385

Stop the insanity now. Vote them out and demand a balanced budget.

There's **NEVER** going to be a BALANCED BUDGET as long as this Country and many others believe in Territorial Rights & WAR!!! It's definitely a **SNOW** JOB & I'm not writing about that **FLUFFY** stuff either!!!

very true: don't "suck it up" and don't break anybody's legs as then you'll be "an eye for an eye, a tooth for a tooth"…and, you'll be going off to jail or prison.

I kan't **STOP!** laughing Mike Hawk **OFF!!!** If it fell off I'd be in a better place butt eye doubt that's going to happen

anytime soon...Namaste: I honor the Spirit
COCKSUCKER that you've becum...you're a **TROOPER**
& it takes Every Kinda People to make the world go
'round...

If a person gets in The White House who isn't white shouldn't the White House being painted black so it can be called The Black House???!!!

Flukers = Fuckers

Fluckers: "With a name like Fluckers it's got to be good."

What's the difference btwn a snowman and a snow-woman? **Snowballs**

I heard what you did for a **Klondike Bar**

Today a man knocked on my door and asked for a small donation towards the local swimming pool: I gave him a glass of water.

Maverick Diamond
Is The **Park & Ride Me** a new program w/ the City of Portland, Maine: how does it work??? Just asking for a friend!
ParkandRideMe221

Ha. Ha. It's only for a select group of a few people **lol** : How you doing?

Bdfrdbud69
Lucky you **Mr. Fab** Hope to go on a trip to warm place after Christmas
MaverickDiamond
If that doesn't pan out then you can always slap yourself **SILLY** & the problem will be **SOLVED**!!!

At least I'm a fun hot mess. Like a train wreck full of pizza, fireworks and glitter.

If you see me smiling that's because I'm thinking evil or naughty. If you see me laughing that's because I've already done it.

Having a Bad Day? You could be a Siamese Twin attached to a Gay brother who has a date and you're the only one with an ass.

I heard the stockings were hung!

They're not up there anymore Walter! A woman refers to her older boobs while her husband is trying to play with them!

Be Honest. What would you like to do with my body? Identify It!

Wonder if the bar has **Black Friday** deals? Like buy one hoe a drink and get her friends clothes half off!!!

I gently slide her panties aside: so that I can fit the rest of the socks in the drawer

The worst word you can use to describe a woman: it's not a cunt, a whore or a slut. It's cow.

My friend Stavros says, "Most men are pigs. They take a shit and want a blow job then split."

"You're a lucky man" is a nice way of telling a guy you'd bang his girlfriend

Laughers Gonna Laugh vs. Haters Gonna Hate: I'll choose the laughter any day of the week!!!

I asked my wife what she wanted for Christmas. "Nothing would make me happier than a diamond necklace." So I bought her nothing

Achieving four mustaches is the final stage of manhood.

I'm not fat: You're just easier to see.

Modern problems require modern solutions: Get hoarders addicted to crack and they'll sell their possessions. They will clean for days non-stop.

You know what beats rock, paper and scissors every time? Tits. Tits win.

Christmas is cancelled! **YOU** told SANTA you have been good all year. He died laughing.

My life in one text: Are you done being sassy? NO

PUSH TO OPEN. If that does not work pull. If both do not work, try the actual **Entrance** to your left.

I never wish death upon anyone who wrongs me. I wish sudden explosive diarrhea while stuck in traffic...with frequent sneezes.

I started a group for men with erectile dysfunction. It was a flop and nobody came.

Lesbians eat what???!!!

Please don't pick on children for believing in Santa. I know there are **Adults** who believe **Fords** are reliable.

There are people who believe that Trump is a good thing ...go figure...

"MayI take your order?" Uh yeah lemme get a long relationship with a side of loyalty & honesty, hold the bullsh!t...

You look pretty today, Jack

Remember when we used to think that people in their 30's were **Adults** and had their shit together? ha ha ha ha ha...

There is no such thing as **bad weather** - just bad clothing.

It's true that dogs are loyal but we cats don't tell the Police where you hide your drugs

"If you touch my balls again, I'll report you for harassment!," said the Christmas tree to the cat.

Wonder if the bar has **Black Friday** deals? Like buy one hoe a drink and get her friends clothes half off.

The phone rings and the wife answers. A pervert breathing heavily says, "I bet you have a tite arse with no hair?" The wife replies, "Yes I do, he's watching t.v....who shall I say is calling."

Can't believe they just let anyone make babies but you gotta have a license to fucking fish.

When I die this is…the best headstone I can ask for: He was an asshole, but he was a funny asshole.

George Harrisson: "Ringo and I are getting' married to each other. But that's a thing you better keep a secret. People would probably think we're queers."

PROMISE ME THE MOON: and lots and lots and lots and lots and lots and lots and lots and lots of laughter!!!!!!!!!!!!!!!!!!!!

The reason a lot of women can't find their Knight In Shining Armor is because she won't let go of that idiot wrapped in Aluminum Foil.

I hope my dick doesn't bone in front of everyone. I only joined to feel cock rub against my ass. The Truth About Wrestling.

BREAKING NEWS: Dalla Cowboys to hire football coach from China. His name is Wee Win Won Soon.

How I feel after Thanksgiving: FAT!!!

Up early in the morning before kids cutting the product: The guy switches **Tootie Fruitees** instead Fruit Loops. Come back to haunt you with the medical bills later on down the road.

I was asked what I look for in a relationship. Apparently, "A Way Out," wasn't the right answer

What a dog says at Thanksgiving: "Mmmmmmm...I smells Tanksgibbin Turkey."

Sometimes being silly with a friend is...the best therapy!

You can't just use, abuse and lose me: I deserve more respect than that!!!

Anybody want to take me out to a baseball game? I like big juicy red Ball Park Franks AND **MORE**!!!

If I'm smacking my food and slurping it that means I'm having sex w/ my food

Miss Mary Bakes A Lot: that's ME!!!

get all the **NEGATIVITY OUT OF YOUR LIFE**: what do you have: PEACE!!!

What's it like to eat guinea pig for the 1st time in Peru? Ashley Lenartson If I was PERUVIAN I might try it...but, I just don't know as I can't related as I'm an AMERICAN!!!

Your approval is not needed: Approval neither desired nor required!!!

This sentence won't take long to read

No self-respecting girl will choose a 6-Pack over six cars...So stop going to the gym & go to work –Robet Mugabe (former PM of Zimbabwe)

Anybody want to see my Christmas Balls: they're sooo...FESTIVE: I decorated them just for **YOU**!!!

Why did the Police arrest the turkey? They suspected **FOWL** play!!!

Are you gonna leave? No I won't. Everybody always leaves. I won't. Did she have an orgy is all I wanna know???!!!

I just bought myself a buttplug that's really WIDE: I don't think it's gonna fit!!!

Billy Fudgepacker: I work for the Keebler Cookie Factory & I love my job. Sometimes, they even let me take a crate of cookies home from work!!!

I have a Big Mac btwn my legs w/ Special Sauce...

Hot times were had by all...enjoy the frigid temperatures & the snow that's cumming down: I guess that God is jerking off AGAIN!!! or, did he comb his hair??? I dunno...

If a man or a woah!man has never been banged in their arse this means technically they're still a VIRGIN!!!

Talk Dirty To Me – Maverick Ashley Lenartson, Ph.D.
Comedy

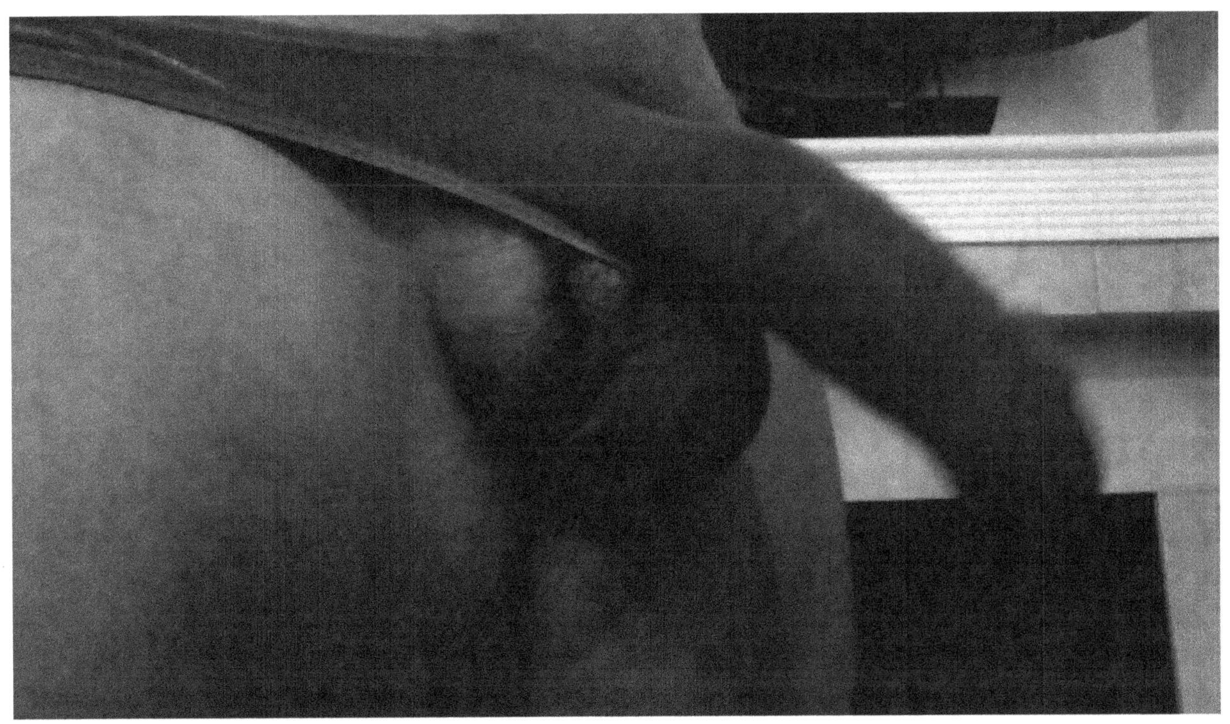

I love the thong: I think I'll buy me one for my oversized Oscar Mayer Wiener for Christmas 2019!!!

2Horny2bhere
Thanks, nice meat you got
MaverickDiamond
why thank you so much: I take care of my meat: may as well tell people I work at a meat factory next time somebody asks me what I do for work...

Good, Better, Best, Outrageous

Are you having a manic episode? Or, is this your normal jovial self???

I don't consider myself mentally ill and would never consider telling anybody that as it's PRIVATE information. I'm just a FFUN guy to be with as I have a very funny dick and a very tasty mouth.
Got any more questions: you'll have to have my people call your people to discuss this situation...it's a very ffunny episode...not even THAT!!!

Tubesteak Slurprise IS the best especially when it cums knocking on your door: you just never know what your gonna get!!!

A man with two buckets of fish was leaving galveston beach well known for its fishing and was stopped by a game warden. The warden asked the man, "Do you have a license to catch those fish?"

A Very Fishy Story

The man replied to the game warden, "No, sir. These are my pet fish."

"Pet fish?!" the warden replied.

"Yes, sir. Every night I take these fish down to this beach and let them swim around for about a half-hour, When I whistle, they all come back, jump back into my buckets, and I take 'em home. We do this every night."

"That's a bunch of hooey," said the warden. "Fish can't do that!"

"No, really! says the man. "Here, I'll show you." And he releases the fish in the ocean.

"Well, I've GOT to see this!" the game warden replied.

The man and the warden stood and waited. After several minutes, the game warden turned to the man and said, "Well?"

"Well, what?" the man asked.

"When are you going to call them back?" the game warden huffs.

"Call who back?" the man asked.

"The FISH."

"What fish?"

Embarrassing = em bare ass ing

Season's Greetings = Seasons Eatings, Pete Schwetty: the thing that I like to bring out at this time of the year are my balls: popcorn, cheese and rum balls...
My mouth is watering just thinking about that. It's been years since I've seen any balls. Whip 'em out. You have some beautiful balls. They're bigger than I expected: look at that Terry the way that they glissen. That's because I make sure they get a little bit of oil.

Fragrant salty nuts

Person calling wrong number: Hello, is Betty Sue there? My grandpa: "She's in bed with a customer can I take your number?"

You should never have a turkey over for lunch: they'll steal your pancakes: after all birds of a feather have to eat, as well.

Grandma once said that "You have to hug the people you don't like so you know how big to dig the hole in the backyard."

An expert in the field without a doubt: ask me any question & I'll do my best to answer it for you!

Sewer blockage pushes waste into 300 New York City homes

j8 hours ago
A water condition caused the backup, pushing human waste into about 300 homes in Jamaica, Queens, officials said."

Ouch, and only 2 days after Thanksgiving dinner.
ReplyReplies (1)

-
- **mike s.** 12 minutes ago

Jamaica , Queens but not in Flushing.

Who doesn't like a fat & juicy piece of meat in their mouth: a steak w/ French fries and fish

Thick & So Juicy: A banana, a thick steak, a cucumber, a milkshake

Tampax named their tampon "**Pearl**" because they go into Clams.

I was in line behind a guy buying condoms and his card got declined. The little old lay behind me whispered, "He got cock blocked by VISA..."

A drug addicts' favorite Christmas song: White Christmas

No arsehole is ever clean unless it's been thoroughly cleaned out with a garden hose!!!

Does anybody know who Mary or Left Palmer is???

Psycho-Anal-yze them

That's right, I'm "straight": straight to bed: I like my meat **HARD UP & TASTY**!!!

Shit = Shirt or Oh Shirt

Piss = Miss the bowl totally as you're wasted

Cunt = You can call a woman this but it's better to call her a Fat or a Fat Pig: that will really get her attention, not cunt, pussy or bitch: those words will also work to get a woman's attention but the one word that most women Universally hate is FAT or Fat Pig: that's a NO! NO!

Mother Fucker = Who here had sex w/ my mother: don't all speak up at once: Tell Your Mama I Said Thanks!!!

Cocksuckers = Those **<u>COCKSUCKERS</u>**: that could be referring to anybody especially in the 50's & 60's!

Tits = Keep Your Eyes Focused on my face, not my tits!!!

Assholes = everybody has two assholes as the lining of your mouth is made of the same lining your asshole is made out of so when you kiss somebody on the lips you're basically kissing their other asshole!

My friend Steve went to a church in his area and the pastor when the service was done said to Steve, "It's awful nice to see you again Steve." Awful???